"If you want to understand what the Bible teaches and what Christians think about these vital matters of life and death, this book is for you!"

John F. Kilner, Professor Emeritus of Bioethics and Contemporary Culture, Trinity Evangelical Divinity School

"Wayne Grudem has faithfully offered a biblical-theological groundwork for making some of the most difficult decisions at the edges of life—its beginning and end. How does one who is committed to the sanctity of every human life approach questions about abortion, euthanasia, and other end-of-life issues? Digest this book to find out."

C. Ben Mitchell, Graves Professor of Moral Philosophy, Union University

T0025432

What the Bible Says about Abortion, Euthanasia, and End-of-Life Medical Issues

Books in This Series

What the Bible Says about Abortion, Euthanasia, and End-of-Life Medical Issues

What the Bible Says about How to Know God's Will

What the Bible Says about Abortion, Euthanasia, and End-of-Life Medical Issues

Wayne Grudem

CROSSWAY®

WHEATON, ILLINOIS

The content of this book has been adapted from "Abortion" and "Euthanasia" in Wayne Grudem, *Christian Ethics: An Introduction to Biblical Moral Reasoning* (Wheaton, IL: Crossway, 2018), 566–605 (chaps. 21–22).

Cover design: Jeff Miller, Faceout Studios
Cover Image: Shutterstock

First printing, 2020
Printed in the United States of America

Trade paperback ISBN: 978-1-4335-6830-5
ePub ISBN: 978-1-4335-6833-6
PDF ISBN: 978-1-4335-6832-9
Mobipocket ISBN: 978-1-4335-6831-2

Library of Congress Cataloging-in-Publication Data

Names: Grudem, Wayne A., author.
Title: What the Bible says about abortion, euthanasia, and end-of-life medical decisions / Wayne Grudem.
Description: Wheaton, Illinois: Crossway, [2020] | Includes bibliographical references and index.
Identifiers: LCCN 2019034880 (print) | LCCN 2019034881 (ebook) | ISBN 9781433568305 (trade paperback) | ISBN 9781433568329 (pdf) | ISBN 9781433568312 (mobi) | ISBN 9781433568336 (epub)
Subjects: LCSH: Christian ethics—Biblical teaching. | Abortion—Religious Aspects—Christianity. | Abortion—Biblical teaching. | Euthanasia—Religious aspects—Christianity. | Euthanasia—Biblical teaching.
Classification: LCC BJ1275 .G78 2020 (print) | LCC BJ1275 (ebook) | DDC 241/.697—dc23
LC record available at https://lccn.loc.gov/2019034880
LC ebook record available at https://lccn.loc.gov/2019034881

Crossway is a publishing ministry of Good News Publishers.

BP		28	27	26	25	24	23	22	21	20
14	13	12	11	10	9	8	7	6	5	4	3	2	1

Contents

INTRODUCTION

What does the Bible teach about the protection of an unborn child?

Is there scientific evidence that the unborn child is a distinct person?

What about abortion in the case of rape or to save the life of the mother?

Is it wrong to put to death a person in great pain who has no hope of recovery?

How can we know when to stop medical treatment near the end of someone's life?

Should the law allow doctors to perform euthanasia when a patient requests it?

This book examines the Bible's teachings on two subjects—abortion and euthanasia—that in many ways are subcategories of the same topic, the protection of human life, both at the beginning of life (in the mother's womb) and at the end of life (in a hospital bed).[1]

---

1. Much of the material in this section has been adapted from Wayne Grudem, *Politics—According to the Bible: A Comprehensive Resource for Understanding*

In the Ten Commandments, we read this:

You shall not murder. (Ex. 20:13)

But this commandment is not confined to the Old Testament. It is repeated several times in the New Testament (see Rom. 1:29; 13:9; 1 Tim. 1:9; James 2:11; 4:2; 1 John 3:12, 15; Rev. 9:21; 16:6; 18:24; 21:8; 22:15; see also Jesus's teaching in Matt. 5:21–26; 15:19; 19:18). The New Testament authors frequently affirm the continuing moral validity of the commandment "You shall not murder."

God is the Creator and sustainer of human life, and human beings are the pinnacle of his creation, for only human beings are said to be created "in the image of God" (Gen. 1:26–27). Therefore, God absolutely forbids human beings to murder one another.[2]

PART 1: ABORTION

Abortion is one of the most controversial topics in society today. Differing views about this topic are related to deeply felt personal convictions about privacy, human sexual behavior, pregnancy, parenthood, and human life itself.

In this section, I will attempt to give an accurate summary of biblical teachings related to abortion and also to

Modern Political Issues in Light of Scripture (Grand Rapids, MI: Zondervan, 2010), 157–78; and *Christian Ethics: An Introduction to Biblical Moral Reasoning* (Wheaton, IL: Crossway, 2018), 566–86, with permission of the publishers.

2. I have elsewhere discussed the fact that the Bible does not view capital punishment or killing an enemy in a just war or in self-defense as "murder," but uses other words to refer to these actions. See Grudem, *Christian Ethics*, 505–6, and chaps. 18, 19, and 20.

represent fairly the arguments of people who disagree with my position. I will use the term *abortion* to mean any action that intentionally causes the death and removal from the womb of an unborn child.

A. BIBLICAL EVIDENCE FOR THE PERSONHOOD OF AN UNBORN CHILD

By far the most powerful argument against abortion is the consideration that the unborn child is a unique person. Several passages in the Bible indicate that an unborn child should be thought of and protected as a person from the moment of conception.

1. Luke 1:41–44. Before the birth of John the Baptist, when his mother, Elizabeth, was in about her sixth month of pregnancy, she was visited by her relative, Mary, who was to become the mother of Jesus. Luke reports:

> And when Elizabeth heard the greeting of Mary, the baby leaped in her womb. And Elizabeth was filled with the Holy Spirit, and she exclaimed with a loud cry, . . . "Behold, when the sound of your greeting came to my ears, *the baby in my womb leaped for joy.*" (Luke 1:41–44)

Under the influence of the Holy Spirit, Elizabeth called the unborn child in the sixth month of pregnancy a "baby" (Greek, *brephos*, "baby, infant"). This is the same Greek word that is used for a child *after* it is born, as when Jesus is called a "baby [*brephos*] lying in a manger" (Luke 2:16; see also Luke 18:15; 2 Tim. 3:15).

Elizabeth also said that the baby "leaped for joy," which attributes personal human activity to him. He was able to hear Mary's voice and somehow, even prior to birth, feel joyful about it. In 2004, researchers at the University of Florida found that unborn children can distinguish their mothers' voices and distinguish music from noise.[3] Another study, reported in *Psychology Today* in 1998, confirmed that babies hear and respond to their mothers' voices while still in the womb, and the mothers' voices have a calming effect on them.[4] More recent research (2013) has shown that babies learn words and sounds in the womb, and retain memories of them after they are born.[5]

2. Psalm 51:5. In the Old Testament, King David sinned with Bathsheba and then was rebuked by Nathan the prophet. Afterward, David wrote Psalm 51, in which he pleads with God, "Have mercy on me, O God, according to your steadfast love" (v. 1). Amidst confessing his sin, he writes:

---

3. University of Florida. "University of Florida Research Adds to Evidence That Unborn Children Hear 'Melody' of Speech," *Science Daily*, Jan. 23, 2004, www.sciencedaily.com/releases/2004/01/040123001433.htm.

4. Janet L. Hopson, "Fetal Psychology," *Psychology Today*, Sept. 1, 1998 (last reviewed June 9, 2016), https://www.psychologytoday.com/articles/199809/fetal-psychology.

5. Eino Partanen et al., "Learning-induced neural plasticity of speech processing before birth," *Proceedings of the National Academy of Sciences of the United States of America*, Sept. 10, 2013, http://www.pnas.org/content/110/37/15145.full. Also see Beth Skwarecki, "Babies Learn to Recognize Words in the Womb," *Science,* Aug. 26, 2013, http://www.sciencemag.org/news/2013/08/babies-learn-recognize-words-womb.

Behold, I was brought forth in iniquity,
   and *in sin did my mother conceive* me. (Ps. 51:5)

David thinks back to the time of his birth and says that he was "brought forth" from his mother's womb as a sinner. In fact, his sinfulness extended back even prior to his birth, for David, under the direction of the Holy Spirit, says, "In sin did my mother conceive me."

Up to this point in the psalm, David is not talking about his mother's sin in any of the preceding four verses, but is talking about the depth of *his own sinfulness* as a human being. Therefore, he must be talking about himself, not about his mother, in this verse as well. He is saying that from the moment of his conception *he* has had a sinful nature. This means that *he thinks of himself as having been a distinct human being, a distinct person, from the moment of his conception*. He was not merely part of his mother's body, but was distinct in his personhood from the time when he was conceived.

3. Psalm 139:13. David also thinks of himself as having been a person while he was growing in his mother's womb, for he says:

You formed my inward parts;
   you knitted *me* together in my mother's womb.
      (Ps. 139:13)

Here also he speaks of himself as a distinct person ("me") when he was in his mother's womb. The Hebrew word translated as "inward parts" is *kilyah*, literally "kidneys," but in contexts such as this it refers to the innermost parts of a person, including his deepest inward thoughts and emotions (see its uses in Pss. 16:7; 26:2; 73:21; Prov. 23:16; Jer. 17:10).

4. Genesis 25:22–23. In an earlier Old Testament example, Rebekah, the wife of Isaac, was pregnant with the twins who were to be named Jacob and Esau. We read:

> The children [Hebrew, *banim*, plural of *ben*, "son"] struggled together within her, and she said, "If it is thus, why is this happening to me?" So she went to inquire of the LORD. And the LORD said to her,
>
> "Two nations are in your womb,
>   and two peoples from within you shall be
>   divided;
> the one shall be stronger than the other,
>   the older shall serve the younger."
>   (Gen. 25:22–23)

Once again, the unborn babies are viewed as "children" within their mother's womb. (The Hebrew word *ben* is the ordinary word used more than forty-nine hundred times in the Old Testament for "son" or, in plural, "sons" or "children.") These twins are viewed as already struggling together. Before the point of birth they are thought of as distinct persons, and their future is predicted.

5. Exodus 21:22–25. For the question of abortion, perhaps the most significant passage of all is found in the specific laws God gave Moses for the people of Israel during the time of the Mosaic covenant. One particular law spoke of the penalties to be imposed if the life or health of a pregnant woman *or her unborn child* was endangered or harmed:

> When men strive together and hit a pregnant woman, so that her children come out, *but there is no harm*, the one who hit her shall surely be fined, as the woman's husband shall impose on him, and he shall pay as the judges determine. But *if there is harm*, then you shall pay life for life, eye for eye, tooth for tooth, hand for hand, foot for foot, burn for burn, wound for wound, stripe for stripe. (Ex. 21:22–25)[6]

This law concerns a situation that arises when men are fighting and one of them accidentally hits a pregnant woman. Neither one of them intends to do this, but as they fight they are not careful enough to avoid hitting her. If that happens, there are two possibilities:

1. If this causes a premature birth but *there is no harm to the pregnant woman or her unborn child*, there is still a penalty: "The one who hit her shall surely be fined" (v. 22). The penalty is for carelessly

---

6. The phrase "so that her children come out" is a literal translation of the Hebrew text, which uses the plural of the common Hebrew word *yeled*, "child," and another very common word, *yātsā'*, which means "go out, come out." The plural "children" is probably the plural of indefiniteness, allowing for the *possibility* of more than one child. Other translations render this as "so that she gives birth prematurely," which is very similar in meaning (so NASB, from the 1999 edition onward; the NIV, TNIV, NET, HCSB, NLT, and NKJV use similar wording).

endangering the life or health of the pregnant woman and her child. We have similar laws in modern society, such as when a person is fined for drunken driving, even though he hit no one with his car. He recklessly endangered human life and health, and he deserves a fine or other penalty.

2. But *"if there is harm"* to either *the pregnant woman* or *her child*, then the penalty is quite severe: "Life for life, eye for eye, tooth for tooth . . ." (vv. 23–24). This means that both the mother and the unborn child are given equal legal protection. The penalty for harming the unborn child is just as great as for harming the mother. Both are treated as persons who deserve the full protection of the law.[7]

---

7. Some translations have adopted an alternative sense of this passage. The NRSV translates it, "When people who are fighting injure a pregnant woman *so that there is a miscarriage, and yet no further harm follows* . . ." (the RSV wording is similar, as was the NASB wording before 1999). In this case, causing a miscarriage and the death of an unborn child results only in a fine. Therefore, some have argued, this passage treats the unborn child as *less worthy* of protection than others in society, for the penalty is less.

But the arguments for this translation are not persuasive. The primary argument is that this translation would make the law similar to a provision in the law code of Hammurabi (written about 1760 BC in ancient Babylon). But such a supposed parallel should not override the meanings of the actual words in the Hebrew text of Exodus. The moral and civil laws in the Bible often differed from those of the ancient cultures around Israel.

In addition, there are two Hebrew words for a "miscarriage" (*shakol*, used in Gen. 31:38; see also Ex. 23:26; Job 21:10; Hos. 9:14; and *nēphel*; see Job. 3:16; Ps. 58:8; Eccles. 6:3), but neither is used here. The word that is used, *yātsā'*, is ordinarily used to refer to the live birth of a child (see Gen. 25:26; 38:29; Jer. 1:5).

Finally, even on this (incorrect) translation, a *fine* is imposed on the person who accidentally causes the death of the unborn child. This implies that *accidentally* causing such a death is still considered morally wrong. Therefore, *intentionally* causing the death of an unborn child would be much more wrong, even according to this translation.

This law is even more significant when seen in the context of other laws in the Mosaic covenant. Where the Mosaic law addressed other cases of someone *accidentally* causing the death of another person, there was no requirement to give "life for life," no capital punishment. Rather, the person who accidentally caused someone else's death was required to flee to one of the six "cities of refuge" until the death of the high priest (see Num. 35:9–15, 22–29). This was a kind of "house arrest," although the person had to stay only within a city rather than within a house for a limited period of time. It was a far lesser punishment than "life for life."

This means that God established for Israel a law code *that placed a higher value on protecting the life of a pregnant woman and her unborn child than the life of anyone else in Israelite society.* Far from treating the death of an unborn child as *less significant* than the death of others in society, this law treated the death of an unborn child or its mother as *more significant* and therefore worthy of more severe punishment. And the law did not make any distinction about the number of months the woman had been pregnant. Presumably it applied from a very early stage in pregnancy, whenever it could be known that the injury inflicted by the men who were fighting caused the death of the unborn child or children.

Moreover, this law applied to a case of *accidental* killing of an unborn child. But if *accidental* killing of an unborn child is so serious in God's eyes, then surely *intentional* killing of an unborn child must be an even worse crime.

6. Luke 1:35: The Incarnation. The angel Gabriel told Mary that she would bear a son, and that this would come about by the power of the Holy Spirit:

> And the angel answered her, "The Holy Spirit will come upon you, and the power of the Most High will overshadow you; therefore the child to be born will be called holy—the Son of God." (Luke 1:35)

Then Elizabeth called Mary "the mother of my Lord" (Luke 1:43) soon after Mary became pregnant. These verses are significant because they mean that the incarnation of Christ did not begin when he was a newborn baby, a small child, a teenager, or an adult man. Rather, the divine nature of God the Son was joined to the human nature of Jesus from the moment of his conception in Mary's womb. From that point on, Jesus Christ was a divine-human person, both God and man. This is significant for the discussion of abortion, because it means that Christ was a genuine human person long before his birth as a baby on the first Christmas.

John Jefferson Davis writes:

> In the New Testament, the incarnation of Jesus Christ is a profound testimony to God's affirmation of the sanctity of prenatal life. . . . His human history, like ours, began at *conception*. . . . The significant point

is that God chose to begin the process of incarnation there, rather than at some other point, thus affirming the significance of that starting point for human life.[8]

Scott Rae agrees:

From the earliest points of life in the womb, Mary and Elizabeth realize that the incarnation has begun. This lends support to the notion that the incarnation began with Jesus's conception and that the Messiah took on human form in all of its stages, embryonic life included.[9]

7. Conclusion. The conclusion from all of these passages is that the Bible teaches that we should think of the unborn child as a person from the moment of conception, and therefore we should give to the unborn child legal protection at least equal to that of others in the society.

8. A Note on Forgiveness. It is likely that many people reading this evidence from the Bible, perhaps for the first time, have already had abortions. Others reading this have encouraged others to have abortions. I cannot minimize or deny the moral wrong involved in these actions, but I can point to the repeated offer of the Bible that God will give forgiveness to those who repent of their sin and trust in Jesus Christ for forgiveness: "If we confess our sins, he

---

8. John Jefferson Davis, *Evangelical Ethics: Issues Facing the Church Today*, 4th ed. (Phillipsburg, NJ: P&R, 2015), 152, emphasis in original.

9. Scott B. Rae, *Moral Choices: An Introduction to Ethics*, 3rd ed. (Grand Rapids, MI: Zondervan, 2009), 130.

is faithful and just to forgive us our sins and to cleanse us from all unrighteousness" (1 John 1:9). Although such sins, like all other sins, deserve God's wrath, Jesus Christ took that wrath on himself as a substitute for all who would believe in him: "He himself bore our sins in his body on the tree, that we might die to sin and live to righteousness. By his wounds you have been healed" (1 Pet. 2:24).

B. SCIENTIFIC EVIDENCE FOR THE PERSONHOOD OF AN UNBORN CHILD

Alongside the biblical testimony about the personhood of the unborn child, scientific evidence also indicates that each child in the womb should be considered to be a unique human person. Dianne Irving, a biochemist and biologist who is a professor at Georgetown University, writes:

> To begin with, scientifically something very radical occurs between the processes of gametogenesis and fertilization—the change from a simple *part* of one human being (i.e., a sperm) and a simple *part* of another human being (i.e., an oocyte—usually referred to as an "ovum" or "egg"), which simply possess "human life," to a new, genetically unique, newly existing, individual, whole living human being (a single-cell embryonic human zygote). That is, upon fertilization, parts of human beings have actually been transformed into something very different from what they were before; they have been changed into a single, whole human being. During the process of fertilization, the sperm

and the oocyte cease to exist as such, and a new human being is produced.

To understand this, it should be remembered that each kind of living organism has a specific number and quality of chromosomes that are characteristic for each member of a species. (The number can vary only slightly if the organism is to survive.) For example, the characteristic number of chromosomes for a member of the human species is 46 (plus or minus, e.g., in human beings with Down's or Turner's syndromes). Every somatic (or, body) cell in a human being has this characteristic number of chromosomes. Even the early germ cells contain 46 chromosomes; it is only their mature forms—the sex gametes, or sperms and oocytes—which will later contain only 23 chromosomes each. Sperms and oocytes are derived from primitive germ cells in the developing fetus by means of the process known as "gametogenesis." Because each germ cell normally has 46 chromosomes, the process of "fertilization" cannot take place until the total number of chromosomes in each germ cell is cut in half. This is necessary so that after their fusion at fertilization the characteristic number of chromosomes in a single individual member of the human species (46) can be maintained. . . .

To accurately see why a sperm or an oocyte are considered as only possessing human life, and not as living human beings themselves, one needs to look at the basic scientific facts involved in the processes of **gametogenesis** and of **fertilization**. It may help to keep in mind that the products of gametogenesis and fertilization are very different. The products of gametogenesis are mature sex gametes with only 23 instead of 46 chromosomes. The product of fertilization is a living human being with 46 chromosomes. Gametogenesis refers to the maturation of germ cells, resulting in gametes. Fertilization refers to the initiation of a new human being.[10]

In other words, the distinct genetic identity of the unborn child shows that he or she is far different (in every single cell of the child's body!) from any part of the mother's own body (for every cell of the mother's body contains the mother's DNA, not the child's).

C. OTHER ARGUMENTS AGAINST ABORTION

The biblical testimony and scientific evidence argue strongly that the unborn child is a person who should be protected by law, and that abortion therefore is wrong and should not be legal. However, not all people are convinced by these arguments. What are some other ways those who accept the personhood of the unborn can argue against abortion?

---

10. Dianne N. Irving, "When Do Human Beings Begin?" *Catholic Education Resource Center*, http://www.catholiceducation.org/en/controversy/abortion/when -do-human-beings-begin.html, emphasis in original. Irving is a former career-appointed bench research biochemist/biologist (National Institutes of Health, National Cancer Institute, Bethesda, MD), an MA and PhD philosopher (Georgetown University, Washington, DC), and professor of the history of philosophy and of medical ethics.

1. Treatment of a Baby after It Is Born. Arguments based on how we treat a child after it is born can have significant persuasive force. For example, would we think it right for our laws to allow a parent to kill a one-year-old child simply because the parent does not want the child or finds the child a difficult burden? If not, should we allow an unborn person to be killed?

2. Ultrasound Images. Modern ultrasound technology gives highly realistic images of the unborn child—images that look so much like a real human person that they have great persuasive force. So great is the resemblance to children after they are born that parents and grandparents often fasten these ultrasound images of unborn children on their refrigerators with magnets! Focus on the Family claims that 78 percent of women who see an ultrasound of their baby in the womb reject abortion.[11] The ministry's "Option Ultrasound" program has been credited with saving more than three hundred and fifty thousand lives from abortion as of 2016.[12]

Because of the powerful evidence of ultrasound images, many abortion advocates try to discourage pregnant women from seeing them. Nancy Keenan, president of the National Abortion Rights Action League Pro-Choice

---

11. See Adam Cohen, "The Next Abortion Battleground: Fetal Heartbeats," *Time,* Oct. 17, 2011, http://ideas.time.com/2011/10/17/the-next-abortion -battleground-fetal-heartbeats/.

12. Leah Jessen, "How This Ultrasound Program Brought Life to 358,000 Babies," *The Daily Signal*, Jan. 7, 2016, http://dailysignal.com/2016/01/07/how-this -ultrasound-program-brought-life-to-358000-babies/.

America in Washington, DC, said, "Politicians should not require a doctor to perform a medically unnecessary ultrasound, nor should they force a woman to view an ultrasound against her will."[13] Abortion advocate William Saletan, writing in *Slate* magazine, said, "Ultrasound has exposed the life in the womb to those of us who didn't want to see what abortion kills. The fetus is squirming, and so are we."[14]

3. The Loss of Millions of Valuable People. Another argument against abortion is the incalculable loss to the nation from the deaths of approximately 1 million babies per year. Since the 1973 Supreme Court decision Roe v. Wade, more than 61 million children have been put to death through abortion.[15] Some of those would now be 47 years old. Others would be 46, 45, and so on, down to approximately 1 million of them who would be in their first year of life.[16]

Many of them by now would be scientists and doctors, engineers and business leaders, entrepreneurs, artists, electricians, poets, carpenters, musicians, farmers, sports figures, political leaders, and so forth. Many of them would be mothers taking care of their own children and fathers

---

13. Quoted in Jennifer Parker, "Bill Would Mandate Ultrasound before Abortion," ABC News, March 16, 2007, http://abcnews.go.com/US/story?id=2958249&page=1&CMP=OTC-RSSFeeds0312.

14. Quoted in Parker, "Bill Would Mandate Ultrasound before Abortion."

15. As of June 28, 2019, the approximate number of abortions performed in the United States since Roe v. Wade is 61,401,741. See www.numberofabortions.com.

16. The number of abortions is decreasing. As of 2015–16, the number of abortions was approximately 926,000. See http://www.nrlc.org/uploads/factsheets/FS01AbortionintheUS.pdf. This is down from a peak of 1.6 million per year in 1990. From 1980 to 1992, the average was over 1.5 million per year.

helping to raise their children. They would be contributing to society in all areas of life—but they never had the chance to be born. They never had the chance to contribute in a positive way to this world.

4. The Instinct of the Mother. A final potent argument is simply an appeal to the instinctive sense a pregnant woman has that what is growing in her womb is not a piece of tissue or merely a part of her body, but is in fact *a baby*. Such an instinct is given even to unbelievers by God himself, for the Bible tells us, with respect to Gentiles "who do not have the Law," that "the work of the Law is *written on their hearts*, while their *conscience* also bears witness, and their conflicting thoughts accuse or even excuse them" (Rom. 2:14–15). This gives us some hope that arguments showing the personhood of the unborn child will eventually be persuasive to the majority of people in a society.

D. COUNTERING ARGUMENTS FOR ABORTION

Those who reject the biblical testimony and the scientific evidence that the unborn child should be treated as a person from the moment of conception present a number of arguments for the permissibility of abortion. In this section, I will summarize and respond to the most prominent of these arguments.

1. Unable to Interact with Others and Survive on Its Own. One objection is that the unborn child is unable to talk or interact with other people or perform moral actions. In addition, it is unable to survive without its mother.

But these factors do not mean that the unborn child is not a person. A newborn is still unable to talk or perform moral actions. This is also true for a person in a coma due to a serious accident. Moreover, a newborn infant is surely unable to survive without its mother. (Some people would say that most junior high students are unable to survive without their mothers!) Such an objection is not persuasive.

2. Birth Defects. Another objection concerns unborn children who are known to have birth defects. Should parents not have the right to abort such children, thus saving themselves much hardship and sparing the child from a life of suffering?

But would we think it right to put such a child to death *after* it is born?

If we have already established that the unborn child should be treated as a person from the moment of conception, then being born or not yet being born should make no difference in our assessment of the child's personhood. If we would not think it right to kill such a child after it is born, then we should not think it right to kill the child before it is born.

Moreover, prior to birth the diagnosis of "possible" or "probable" birth defects can be in error. Sometimes a child is born perfectly normal after such a diagnosis. Many birth defects are very small and have no significant impact on the child's life. And even when a birth defect is quite significant (for example, Down syndrome), the child can still lead a happy life and bring much joy and blessing to his or her own family and to many others.[17] In such cases Christians should be encouraged to trust in God's wise providence and his sovereign direction of their lives. The Lord said to Moses, "Who has made man's mouth? Who makes him mute, or deaf, or seeing, or blind? Is it not I, the LORD?" (Ex. 4:11). On one occasion, Jesus saw a man who had been blind from birth:

> His disciples asked him, "Rabbi, who sinned, this man or his parents, that he was born blind?" Jesus answered, "It was not that this man sinned, or his parents, but that the works of God might be displayed in him." (John 9:2–3)

Randy Alcorn quotes an example of a medical school professor who presented the following case study and asked students what they would do:

> The father had syphilis and the mother had tuberculosis. Of four previous children, the first was blind, the second died, the third was both deaf and dumb, and the fourth had tuberculosis. What would you advise the woman to do when she finds she is pregnant again?

---

17. Robertson McQuilkin and Paul Copan raise a point that people often overlook: "Blessing and benefit come not only to the handicapped, but also to their caregivers, many of whom deepen in their compassion and even their courage while tending to the needs of others." *An Introduction to Biblical Ethics: Walking in the Way of Wisdom*, 3rd ed. (Downers Grove, IL: InterVarsity Press, 2014), 380.

One student answered, "I would advise an abortion." Then the professor said, "Congratulations. . . . You have just killed Beethoven."[18]

3. Pregnancies Resulting from Rape or Incest. If a child has been conceived through rape or incest, we must recognize the genuine pain and hardship experienced by the mother, who is involuntarily pregnant, perhaps at a very young age. Christians who know of such situations should be ready to give encouragement and support in many ways.

But once again the question must be asked: Would we think it right to kill a baby conceived through rape or incest *after* it is born? Most people would say certainly not. Such a child does not lose its right to live because of the circumstances of its conception. Therefore, we should not think it right to kill the child *before* it is born either. The rape that occurred was not the fault of the child, and the child should not be put to death because of someone else's crime. "Fathers shall not be put to death because of their children, nor shall children be put to death because of their fathers. Each one shall be put to death for his own sin" (Deut. 24:16; cf. Ezek. 18:20). In addition, pregnancies resulting from rape or incest are quite rare, account-

---

18. Randy Alcorn, *ProLife Answers to ProChoice Arguments* (Portland, OR: Multnomah, 1992), 175. By quoting this argument, I do not wish to imply that only the lives of famous composers are worth saving, but just the opposite: all human lives are worth saving both because we are created in the image of God and because we can never know in advance how much good a child will do in his or her lifetime, if allowed to live. Beethoven, who was born in circumstances that were far from ideal, is simply a vivid illustration of the second point. (See Grudem, *Christian Ethics*, 141–43, 151, on the importance of evaluating the results of our actions.)

ing for at most 1 percent of all abortions,[19] but probably much less than that.

Alcorn points out that well-known gospel singer Ethel Waters was born as a result of a pregnancy that occurred when her mother was raped at age 12.[20] There are doubtless other people today who lead useful, productive, fulfilling lives even though their births were the result of the horrible crime of rape.[21] We should not justify taking the life of the unborn child in such cases.

4. Abortion to Save the Life of the Mother. According to the Centers for Disease Control, abortion carried out to save the life of the mother is extremely rare (less than 0.118 percent of all abortions).[22] A more recent study in the United Kingdom found that only 0.006 percent of all abortions there were to save the life of the mother.[23] Such a situation is different from the others we considered above,

---

19. According to the Alan Guttmacher Institute, the research arm of Planned Parenthood, less than 0.5 percent of abortions in 2004 were performed on victims of rape. See Lawrence B. Finer et al., "Reasons U.S. Women Have Abortions: Quantitative and Qualitative Perspectives," *Perspectives on Sexual and Reproductive Health* 37, no. 3 (2005): 114, https://www.guttmacher.org/sites/default/files/pdfs/journals/3711005.pdf.

20. Alcorn, *ProLife Answers*, 179.

21. An excellent student in one of my seminary classes confided to me privately that after he became an adult he learned from his parents that his legal father, who had brought him up from birth, was not his biological father, but had married the student's mother after she had been raped by another man. At the time the student told me this, he had already completed several years of fruitful ministry.

22. Jeani Chang et al., "Pregnancy-Related Mortality Surveillance—United States, 1991–1999," Centers for Disease Control and Prevention, *Morbidity and Mortality Weekly Report*, Feb. 21, 2003, www.cdc.gov/mmwr/preview/mmwrhtml/ss5202a1.htm.

23. According to The Parliamentary Under-Secretary of State, Department of Health (Earl Howe). See http://www.publications.parliament.uk/pa/ld201213/ldhansrd/text/120719w0001.htm#12071972000444.

because here the choice is between the loss of one life (the baby's) and the loss of two lives (both the baby's and the mother's).

I cannot see a reason to say that abortion in this situation would be morally wrong, and in fact I believe it would be morally right for doctors to save the life that *can* be saved and take the life of the unborn child. This scenario is significantly different from most abortion cases, because in this instance removing the unborn child from the mother's body (for example, from the fallopian tube in the case of an ectopic pregnancy) results from *directly intending to save the life of the mother*, not from *directly intending to take the child's life*. If the medical technology exists to save the child's life in such cases, then of course the child's life should also be saved. But if abortion is necessary to save the mother's life, this would seem to be the only situation in which abortion is morally justified.

Therefore, it seems right to me that all mainstream pro-life proposals for legal restrictions on abortion have included an exception to save the life of the mother. But in politics, proponents of "abortion rights" too often lump together "life" and "health," and declare that they are willing to restrict abortion "except to save the *life or health* of the mother." Then in actual practice, "health" becomes defined so broadly in legal precedents that it also includes "mental health," including freedom from excessive distress; thus, "except to save the life *or health* of the mother" in practice means abortion is allowed whenever the mother wants to obtain one.

In fact, Doe v. Bolton, the companion case to Roe v. Wade, defined maternal "health" as "all factors—physical, emotional, psychological, familial, and the woman's age—relevant to the well-being of the patient." These factors are so vague and open-ended that almost any reason can be cited to allow an abortion in the second and third trimesters. Therefore, abortion is legal—and cannot be prohibited—in the fourth, fifth, sixth, seventh, eighth, or ninth month of pregnancy if any of the reasons is invoked.[24]

E. WHAT LAWS SHOULD GOVERNMENTS ENACT REGARDING ABORTION?

One of the fundamental responsibilities of a government is to *protect the lives* of the people it governs, for if government is to punish those who do evil and to prevent them from harming the innocent,[25] then a government certainly must protect its people from the ultimate harm of being killed.[26] If unborn children are considered persons, then surely government should protect their lives.[27] In fact, it is *especially* the weak and helpless, those without other means of protection, who should be the objects of governmental protections:

---

24. This Supreme Court case is Doe v. Bolton, 41 U.S. 179, 192 (1973); see http://caselaw.findlaw.com/us-supreme-court/410/179.html.

25. See Grudem, *Christian Ethics*, 428.

26. See Grudem *Christian Ethics*, 507–8.

27. As for penalties that would apply to those who break the law, that would be determined by the legislature in each state. (Prior to Roe v. Wade, most state penalties were against the doctor who performed the abortion rather than the woman who received the abortion.)

Give justice to the weak and fatherless; maintain the right of the afflicted and the destitute. Rescue the weak and needy; deliver them from the hand of the wicked. (Ps. 82:3–4)

Therefore, I would recommend the following governmental policies and laws regarding abortion:[28]

1. Governments should enact laws prohibiting abortions except to save the life of the mother.[29]
2. No government policies should promote or fund abortions.
3. No government policies should compel people to participate in abortions or to dispense drugs that cause abortions.
4. No government funding or support should be given to the process of creating human embryos for the purpose of destroying them in medical research.

However, we must also recognize that in the United States at the present time, the Congress *has no power* to pass a law prohibiting abortions at any stage of pregnancy.

---

28. Elsewhere I have discussed the current legal situation in the United States and the reasons for several specific recommendations concerning government laws about abortion. See Grudem, *Politics—According to the Bible*, 157–78. What follows in this section is a summary of that longer discussion.

29. What if a "compromise" law were proposed that would prohibit abortions except to save the life of the mother or in cases of rape or incest? I think that Christians should support such legislation, since it would prohibit roughly 99 percent of the abortions that are occurring today. After such a law is passed, perhaps modifications could be made to the law in the future, if public sentiment would support it. But even such a law would do a tremendous amount of good in protecting the lives of the vast majority of unborn children who today are being put to death.

And the fifty state legislatures *have no power* to pass any law prohibiting abortion.[30] (The prohibition on partial-birth abortion, which survived Supreme Court scrutiny, is the only exception.) This is because every law prohibiting abortion has been struck down by the Supreme Court as "unconstitutional" because the court says such laws violate the Constitution's guarantee of a right to abortion![31] And this is the decision of the court even though the Constitution itself says nothing about abortion.[32]

The blunt reality is that no laws prohibiting abortions can be enacted in the United States until the Supreme Court overturns Roe v. Wade. Therefore, Christians who genuinely seek significant changes in the abortion laws in the United States should support prolife candidates for office, especially for the presidency and the Senate, because the president alone nominates Supreme Court justices, and the Senate must approve those nominations before a nominee can join the court.

---

30. However, the situation in the United States may be changing (I am writing this note in August 2019). Several states have passed laws prohibiting abortion after a certain stage in pregnancy, such as after a heartbeat is detected. These laws have faced legal challenges and are now working their way through the courts. The recently established "originalist" majority on the Supreme Court (with the additions of Justices Neil Gorsuch and Brett Kavanaugh) is a fact that leads many court observers to expect that Roe v. Wade will be modified or overturned when these cases reach the Supreme Court.

31. Under Roe v. Wade and the companion case Doe v. Bolton, the Supreme Court allowed abortion for the mother's health, including emotional and psychological health, which effectively allows abortion at any time in the nine months of pregnancy (see the discussion earlier in this book).

32. For an explanation of why Roe v. Wade was based on an illegitimate "interpretation" of the U.S. Constitution (it was actually a rewriting of part of the Constitution), see Grudem, *Politics—According to the Bible*, 133–34.

F. OBJECTIONS TO LAWS RESTRICTING ABORTION

Here are some objections that people have raised against the idea of prohibiting abortions:

1. "These Laws Are a Wrongful Restriction of Freedom." Some people will argue that a law prohibiting abortions wrongfully restricts individual human freedom. Shouldn't the decision about whether to carry a baby to full term and give birth be made by the mother herself? How can it be right to say that the law should force a woman to endure a pregnancy and bear a child that she does not want? Isn't individual freedom a foundational principle of this country? Sometimes people will say, "I think that's a decision that should be up to the mother and her doctor, and the mother should be free to decide as she thinks best."

Individual freedom is of course important and should be protected. But the real question is not freedom in the abstract but what *appropriate restrictions* the law should place on individual freedom. Laws already restrict freedom in many ways that people accept. The law does not allow me the freedom to drive while intoxicated, to steal my neighbor's car, to beat up someone I don't like, or to fire a gun inside the city limits—and surely it does not allow parents to put their living children to death. So the question is not human freedom, but whether the law should allow people *freedom to take their child's life.* If the unborn child is considered a human person, the question is whether the government should allow people to commit murder against their own children. Certainly it should not.

2. "All Children Should Be Wanted Children." This is another popular phrase used by politicians who advocate for unrestricted abortion. The benefit of allowing abortions, some people say, is that it gives mothers the freedom not to bear children they really don't want, children that might grow up to be neglected, abused, and poorly cared for. Why not allow abortions so that only mothers who really *want* their children will have them?

But if we consider the unborn child to be a person, then this argument is merely another way of saying that people should be allowed to kill other people that they do not want to care for. In particular, parents should be able to kill the children that they do not want to care for.

Once a child is born, would we say that a parent who does not "want" to care for that child any longer should have the right to put him or her to death because "all children should be wanted children"? Surely not. This is a horrible thought, but it is simply the logical conclusion of the "all children should be wanted children" argument. This is really a morally bankrupt argument, one that so devalues human life that it values a mother's desire for convenience more highly than the right to life of a child made in the very image of God.

3. "I'm Personally against Abortion, but I Don't Support Laws against Abortion." This argument is made by a number of politicians who do not want to appear to be *supporting* the idea of killing unborn children, but who still are committed to protecting the *legal* right of women to have abortions if they choose. Presumably, if they were asked for advice by a pregnant woman, they would tell her that they would *personally recommend* that she not get an abortion. But the decision, of course, is still up to her.

This argument fails to understand the difference between personal moral persuasion and governmental laws. If we really believe that an action is taking innocent human lives, then we will not be content to depend on moral influence to stop it. This position would be similar to saying, "*I'm personally opposed to drunken driving, and I wouldn't personally recommend* drunken driving, but I don't support having laws against it, because I think *individual drivers should have the right to decide for themselves* whether to drive when drunk." The fact of the matter is that, apart from legal enforcement by the government, many people will foolishly decide to drive while intoxicated and will actually kill other people through their wrongful choices. Government is instituted by God to protect us from such wrongdoing by others.

This argument is, in fact, a subtle attempt at changing the subject. The subject under dispute is not *personal preferences* of individuals, but what *the laws of a government* should prohibit. Just as we would not say, "I'm personally opposed to murder, but I don't think there should be any laws against murder," so it seems naive and, I think, misleading to say, "I'm personally opposed to abortion, but I don't think that there should be laws against abortion."

4. "We Should Reduce the Causes of Abortion but Not Have Laws against Abortion." A similar position to "I'm personally against abortion, but I don't support laws against abortion" is that of Jim Wallis, expressed in his book *God's Politics*. Wallis says that "the abortion rate in America is much too high for a good and healthy society that respects both women and children," and he recommends "really targeting the problems of teen pregnancy and adoption reform, which are so critical to reducing abortion, while offering real support for women, especially low-income women, at greater risk for unwanted pregnancies."[33]

But this is just changing the subject. The subject under discussion is *laws* about abortion. The specific question is: *What should the laws about abortion be?* Should laws prohibit abortion (with certain exceptions) or not? Saying we should try to reduce teen pregnancy in order to stop abortion is like saying we should support Alcoholics Anonymous in order to stop drunken driving, or we should support job creation to stop stealing, or we should support anger-management clinics to stop murder. Those are helpful social programs, but they alone will not stop those crimes.

What Wallis refuses to say in *God's Politics* is that we should have *laws* that prohibit women from taking the lives

---

33. Jim Wallis, *God's Politics: Why the Right Gets It Wrong and the Left Doesn't Get It* (New York: HarperCollins, 2005), 299–300.

of their unborn children. Our laws should protect human life. The main difference between conservatives and liberals on abortion is how they answer this question: *Should it be against the law to kill your unborn child?*

I believe it should be against the law (except to save the mother's life). Certainly we *also* should give support to low-income women who are pregnant, but both sides agree on this. The solution is "both-and"—both maternal support and laws. But Wallis will not say "both-and." When asked *what the laws should be*, he and others simply change the subject to maternal support. They will not support laws to prohibit abortion.

5. "Everyone Who Opposes Abortion Should Adopt a 'Consistent Ethic of Life.'" How can some evangelicals vote for proabortion candidates for the U.S. Senate or for president? One approach is to change the subject from discussing laws about abortion to saying we should give more support to women who are pregnant, and so reduce abortion (see discussion in the previous section). Another common approach is also exemplified by Wallis. He says that Christians should support "a consistent ethic of life," but that *neither political party* is satisfactory in this area. He defines this ethic as including "the life issues" of "abortion, euthanasia, capital punishment, nuclear weapons, poverty, and racism." He calls these "critical components of a consistent ethic of life."[34] Then he says:

---

34. Wallis, *God's Politics*, 300–301.

The tragedy is that in America today, one can't vote for a consistent ethic of life. Republicans stress some of the life issues, Democrats some of the others, while both violate the seamless garment of life on several vital matters.[35]

In other words, no party practices "a consistent ethic of life" (according to Wallis) on all of these issues, and therefore people shouldn't think that they should vote for Republicans because of the abortion issue, because there are other "life" issues on which the Democratic position is better.

But Christians should understand what Wallis is doing here. He is changing the subject from laws prohibiting abortion to laws about a whole range of things, and he is claiming that a *truly Christian* prolife position would include such policies as opposition to capital punishment, opposition to nuclear weapons, and increased government help for the poor (as he explains elsewhere in his book *God's Politics*). The effect of this argument by Wallis is to downplay the importance of the abortion issue by saying that these are all "life" issues.

I agree that it is important to consider all the issues that politicians in both parties stand for before deciding how to vote. But it is hard to see how any issue could be more important than stopping the wrongful murder of more than 1 million innocent unborn children year after year. I think Wallis

---

35. Wallis, *God's Politics*, 301.

is wrong to diminish this issue by lumping it with a whole basket of other controversial and complicated questions.

In addition, many Christians sincerely disagree with Wallis about capital punishment, national defense, and solutions to poverty. Wallis's phrase "a consistent ethic of life" is a misleading slogan that attempts to make people think that his pacifist views on capital punishment and war, his support for government redistribution of wealth, and his own solutions to racial discrimination are the truly "prolife" positions. This dilutes the argument about the biblical teaching against abortion by enlarging the discussion to include many other disputed issues. This sleight-of-hand argument should not blind us to the plain fact that every vote for every proabortion candidate for president or Congress undeniably has the effect of continuing to permit 1 million abortions per year in the United States.

6. "Christians Should Not Try to Impose Their Moral Standards on Other People." People who make this objection would usually say that it's fine for Christians to think that abortion is wrong *for themselves*, but they have no right to try to force that conviction on others who do not have a Christian viewpoint.

In response, it must be said that many of our laws are based on moral convictions that are held by the vast majority of the population. The laws against murder are based on the moral conviction that murder is wrong. The laws against stealing are based on the moral conviction that stealing is wrong. Laws against polygamy and incest are based on moral convictions that those practices are wrong. Laws against sexual harassment or adults having sex with minors are based on moral convictions that those actions are wrong. We could multiply examples by the thousands from all areas of the law.

Which moral standards support laws against abortions? There are two: (1) people should not be allowed to murder other people and (2) the unborn child should be considered a human person and therefore should be protected as a human person. No doubt almost everyone would agree on the first point. So the question really involves the second point, whether the unborn child should be considered a human person worthy of legal protection.

In our system of government, Christians cannot *impose* their moral convictions on anyone. But everyone in the nation is free to attempt to *persuade* others about the moral convictions that should be the basis for various laws. So instead of "Christians should not try to impose their moral standards on others," a more accurate way of phrasing this objection is "Christians should not try to persuade others that the unborn child is a human person who deserves the legal protections due to all human persons."

Of course, when the objection is stated that way, hardly anyone would agree with it. Surely our nation was founded on the freedom of citizens *to speak about their convictions and try to persuade others*, and thereby to try to influence laws. In fact, the First Amendment *guarantees* freedom of speech and freedom of the press, assuring us that people of all persuasions are free to argue and attempt to persuade others about what kinds of laws should be made.

Finally, Christians should not view their conviction about the personhood of the unborn child as "*our* moral conviction." We did not make it up out of our own minds, but found it written in the Bible. And the Bible presents it as not mere human opinion, but the moral standard of God himself, by which he holds all people in every nation accountable (see the discussion in Grudem, *Christian Ethics*, 434–35).

It does seem right for Christians to attempt to persuade others that the moral standards found in the Bible are correct and should be used in human government. It was on the basis of this conviction that Paul could reason with the Roman governor Felix "about *righteousness* and self-control and the coming judgment" (Acts 24:25). It was on this basis that John the Baptist "reproved" Herod the tetrarch "for all the *evil things* that Herod had done" (Luke 3:19). And it was on this basis that Daniel warned King Nebuchadnezzar of Babylon about his "sins" and "iniquities" (Dan. 4:27), and Jonah warned the entire city of Nineveh to repent (see Jonah 3:4; see also the discussion of Christian influence on government in Grudem, *Christian Ethics*, 468–77).

G. THE IMPORTANCE OF THIS ISSUE

The Old Testament contains sober warnings to a nation that allowed people to put their children to death. In imitation of the practices of other nations, some of the people of Israel had begun "to burn their sons and their daughters in the fire" (Jer. 7:31), which referred to putting their live children into a fire to sacrifice them to Molech and other pagan gods. For allowing this practice to continue, God issued a severe warning of judgment through the prophet Jeremiah:

> For the sons of Judah have done evil in my sight, declares the LORD. . . . And they have built the high places of Topheth, which is in the Valley of the Son of Hinnom, *to burn their sons and their daughters in the fire*, which I did not command, nor did it come into my mind. Therefore, behold, the days are coming, declares the LORD, when it will no more be called Topheth, or the Valley of the Son of Hinnom, but the Valley of Slaughter; for they will bury in Topheth, because there is no room elsewhere. And the dead bodies of this people will be food for the birds of the air, and for the beasts of the earth, and none will frighten them away. And I will silence in the cities of Judah and in the streets of Jerusalem the voice of mirth and the voice of gladness, the voice of the bridegroom and the voice of the bride, *for the land shall become a waste*. (Jer. 7:30–34)

The troubling question with regard to the United States (and many other countries today) concerns the direction the nation has taken. It has willingly chosen to be represented and governed by elected officials who resolutely champion the right of a woman to take the life of her unborn child. What will God's evaluation of our nation be in light of such decisions? Or do we not think that God is still sovereign over the affairs of nations?

PART 2: EUTHANASIA

The word *euthanasia* is derived from the Greek words *eu* ("good") and *thanatos* ("death"), and therefore people sometimes understand it to mean "good death," a rather misleading understanding of the term. Sometimes this procedure is popularly called "mercy killing," another term that is misleading in portraying such an action in a positive way. *Euthanasia* is simply the act of intentionally ending the life of a person who is elderly, terminally ill, or suffering from some incurable injury or disease.[36]

This issue often comes to focus in the case of terminally-ill patients who are experiencing chronic pain and therefore no longer want to live and may even wish to be put to death. It also is a question in the case of people who have lost much or most of their mental capacities because of a coma or severe dementia, or patients who appear to have no reasonable human hope of recovery from a severe injury or illness. What is the morally right thing to do in such cases?

A. BIBLICAL TEACHING

1. Exodus 20:13: The Sixth Commandment. The primary biblical teaching in this regard is found in the sixth commandment:

You shall not murder. (Ex. 20:13)

---

36. This section has been adapted from Grudem, *Politics—According to the Bible*, 178–86, and *Christian Ethics*, 587–605, with permission of the publishers.

This commandment, which is affirmed in the New Testament in Matthew 19:18 and Romans 13:9, applies to all human beings created in the image of God. It does not say, "You shall not murder, except when a person is more than eighty or ninety years old," or, "You shall not murder, except when a very ill person wants to be murdered."

Just as the command against murder prohibits abortion in the very early stages of human life, so the command against murder also prohibits the intentional killing of a person in the final stages of human life.

As I have explained in more detail elsewhere,[37] the word translated as "murder" in Exodus 20:13 refers to both premeditated murder (which is communicated by the English word *murder*) and also any accidental causing of a person's death through negligence or carelessness. The term is always applied to the murder of human beings, not of animals. Therefore, this biblical command prohibits taking the life of another person, even if that person is elderly, terminally ill, or in great pain.

2. Second Samuel 1:1–16: The Death of Saul. One other passage of special significance is 2 Samuel 1:1–16. King Saul had recently died in battle, in effect making David king. A few days after the battle in which Saul had died, a man came to David and claimed that he had found Saul gravely wounded and that Saul had begged the man to kill him, so the man had done so. In several ways this was

---

37. See Grudem, *Christian Ethics*, 505.

an act of "euthanasia." Yet David's response was to order capital punishment for the man who had done this. Here is the story:

> After the death of Saul, when David had returned from striking down the Amalekites, David remained two days in Ziklag. And on the third day, behold, a man came from Saul's camp, with his clothes torn and dirt on his head. And when he came to David, he fell to the ground and paid homage. David said to him, "Where do you come from?" And he said to him, "I have escaped from the camp of Israel." And David said to him, "How did it go? Tell me." And he answered, "The people fled from the battle, and also many of the people have fallen and are dead, and Saul and his son Jonathan are also dead." Then David said to the young man who told him, "How do you know that Saul and his son Jonathan are dead?" And the young man who told him said, "By chance I happened to be on Mount Gilboa, *and there was Saul leaning on his spear, and behold, the chariots and the horsemen were close upon him.* And when he looked behind him, he saw me, and called to me. And I answered, 'Here I am.' And he said to me, 'Who are you?' I answered him, 'I am an Amalekite.' And he said to me, '*Stand beside me and kill me, for anguish has seized me*, and yet my life still lingers.' *So I stood beside him and killed him, because I was sure that he could not live after he had fallen.* And I took the crown that was on his head and the armlet that was on his arm, and I have brought them here to my lord."

Then David took hold of his clothes and tore them, and so did all the men who were with him. And they mourned and wept and fasted until evening for Saul and for Jonathan his son and for the people of the LORD and for the house of Israel, because they had fallen by the sword. And David said to the young man who told him, "Where do you come from?" And he answered, "I am the son of a sojourner, an Amalekite." David said to him, "How is it you were not afraid to put out your hand to destroy the LORD's anointed?" Then David called one of the young men and said, *"Go, execute him." And he struck him down so that he died.* And David said to him, "Your blood be on your head, for your own mouth has testified against you, saying, 'I have killed the LORD's anointed.'" (2 Sam. 1:1–16)

This narrative has several similarities to modern situations in which people sometimes say euthanasia is justified:

1. The patient (Saul) appeared to be terminally injured, with no reasonable human hope of recovery. (He had fallen on his own sword in an attempt to commit suicide: see 1 Sam. 31:4–5.)
2. The patient was in extreme pain, and if he did not die, he faced the prospect of even more suffering.
3. The patient clearly requested, even begged, that someone would put him to death.
4. This request was also a command from the head of government at that time, because Saul was still the king.

But David, who at that time is clearly portrayed as a man after God's "own heart" (1 Sam. 13:14; cf. Acts 13:22), declares that this man who has killed Saul is worthy of capital punishment. In other words, the person who carried out euthanasia is *guilty of murder*.

Three objections may be brought against this interpretation:

First, this story about the Amalekite messenger killing Saul is not mentioned in 1 Samuel 31:3–6, where Saul's death is first reported. Therefore the Amalekite messenger may be making up this story to convince David that he has killed Saul, who is David's enemy.

However, this idea does not nullify the force of this narrative, because even if the story is not true, *David accepts it as true and passes judgment on the man based on the story*. David condemns him based on his own confession of guilt. And thus the narrative of Scripture portrays the decision of this wise king, a man after God's own heart, as *an appropriate and morally right judgment* on the man who has carried out euthanasia.

In addition, the Amalekite messenger actually has the crown and the armlet that Saul had been wearing, and he knows that Saul had fallen on his own sword, so it is quite certain that the man was there in the vicinity of Saul when Saul was dying. Therefore, it is certainly possible that his story is entirely true and simply was not included in the summary of Saul's death in 1 Samuel 31. In fact, verse 4 of that chapter does not specify that Saul killed himself, but that he tried to do so: "Saul took his own sword and fell upon it." The next verse says that at some later point Saul's armor-bearer "saw that Saul was dead," but it allows for the Amalekite to end Saul's life before that. In any case, the events probably occurred very quickly in the heat of battle.

Second, this case is unique because Saul was king, and David refers to him as "the LORD's anointed" (2 Sam. 1:14). Therefore, it should not be used to establish a general principle that euthanasia is wrong, but only the specific application that assassination of a king is wrong.

However, this objection is not persuasive, because the wrongfulness of murder does not depend on the status or rank of the victim. Murder is wrong because God prohibits it (Ex. 20:13), and more specifically because it is the taking of the life of a person made in the image of God (see Gen. 9:5–6). A king does not possess a greater share of the image of God than others who do not happen to be king! All human beings share equally in the status of being created in the image of God (Gen. 1:27). Therefore, if it is wrong to kill a terminally-ill king who requests it, then it is also wrong to kill anyone else who requests it.

Third, the sin of the Amalekite messenger was not murder, but rebellion against the king, who was God's anointed.

However, this interpretation does not match the actual words of the text, for David does not put the man to death for rebellion, but for murder (2 Sam. 1:14, 16). And in fact, at the time this happened, the Amalekite was not rebelling against the king, but was actually obeying what the king commanded. The sin was murder, and David punishes it accordingly.

Therefore, this narrative gives significant confirmation of the rightness of applying "You shall not murder" to the question of euthanasia.

The conclusion is that both Exodus 20:13 and 2 Samuel 1:1–16 indicate that it is morally wrong to actively take the life of a terminally-ill person who is suffering and who asks to be put to death.

B. THE CRUCIAL DIFFERENCE BETWEEN KILLING AND LETTING DIE

A clear distinction must be made between "killing" and "letting die." *Killing* is actively doing something to a patient that hastens or causes his or her death. On the other hand, *letting die* is passively allowing someone to die from other causes, without interfering with that process.[38] In the first case, the cause of death is the action taken by another person. In the second case, the cause of death is the disease, injury, or aging process that has already been occurring in the person who dies. While the Bible prohibits actively kill-

---

38. Sometimes actively killing a suffering person is called "active euthanasia" to distinguish it from letting someone die (which is sometimes called "passive euthanasia"). I have decided not to use these terms in this chapter because they wrongly make the two actions sound similar, blurring the crucial moral distinction between killing someone and letting someone die.

ing someone, in the case of letting someone die the moral decision is more complex.

Sometimes it is clearly wrong to let a person die. We *should* intervene and try to help a person recover, and *not* passively allow the person to die, when (1) there is a reasonable human hope of recovery and (2) we are able to help. This would be obeying Jesus's teaching "You shall love your neighbor as yourself" (Matt. 22:39) and his command "So whatever you wish that others would do to you, do also to them, for this is the Law and the Prophets" (Matt. 7:12). Moreover, in the parable of the good Samaritan, Jesus implicitly condemned the priest and the Levite who neglected to do what they could to help a badly injured man (see Luke 10:30–37).

On the other hand, in cases where (1) there is no reasonable human hope of recovery (sometimes called a situation of "futility"), and (2) it is the patient's wish to be allowed to die, and/or (3) we are unable to help (such as when a person is trapped in a burning car or when the expense of necessary medical treatments is more than we can bear), *then it may be right to allow the person to die*. This is morally distinct from actively murdering a person.

Allowing someone to die may include *not starting* a medical life-support system (such as an artificial respirator) or *stopping* a life-support system. Although many people in modern secular societies harbor a deep fear of death, Christians need not fear death. Sometimes in Scripture we see examples of people realizing that their death is near, and then they simply trust God and yield their lives into his hands (see Luke 2:29; 23:46; Acts 7:59; see also Gen. 49:33; 1 Cor. 15:55–57; Heb. 2:15;).

My own personal decision may be helpful at this point. If a circumstance should arise where I am facing a terminal illness, and there is no reasonable human hope of recovery, and I am no longer conscious—no longer able to make my wishes known and probably no longer able even to consciously pray—in such a situation, would I want a large amount of effort and expense put forth to keep me from dying and therefore to keep me out of heaven? Certainly not.

The example of the apostle Paul is a good one. He said he could see benefits in remaining alive and also great benefits in dying and going to be with Christ, but his affirmation of these two "good" alternatives leads us to conclude that he certainly would not have wanted to be somehow suspended between the two for weeks or even months. He wanted one or the other, either life or death:

> It is my eager expectation and hope that I will not be at all ashamed, but that with full courage now as always Christ will be honored in my body, *whether by life or by death*. For to me to live is Christ, and to die is gain. If I am to live in the flesh, that means fruitful labor for me. Yet which I shall choose I cannot tell. I am hard pressed between the two. My desire is to depart and be with Christ, for that is far better. But to remain in the flesh is more necessary on your account. (Phil. 1:20–24)

It seems to me, however, that providing nutrition and hydration is different from an artificial life-support system. What if a patient is unconscious or so weak that he cannot feed himself? Should he be given a feeding tube to provide food and water (often called "nutrition and hydration")? My own conviction is that we *should* provide ongoing nutrition and hydration if we are able to do so. I believe this because it seems to me to be an ordinary expression of Christian mercy and compassion to prevent the patient from dying of thirst or starvation rather than dying from the disease or injury itself. By analogy, if the patient had been in a severe car accident and both arms had been broken, and he was therefore unable to feed himself, we would certainly want to provide nutrition and hydration. Therefore, I think we should also do this when the patient's inability to feed himself is caused not by broken arms but by being unconscious.[39]

However, I recognize that at times the exact medical situation is more complex, and a decision about nutrition and hydration (especially nutrition) may be more difficult. On April 21, 2016, the Christian Medical & Dental Associations issued a thoughtful statement that takes into account more of these complexities.[40] The statement recommends

---

39. J. P. Moreland argues, I think rightly, "If food and water are withdrawn or withheld, then death is intentionally brought about directly and immediately by that act itself. In such a case, disease does not directly kill; the act of forgoing treatment directly kills. Thus, a decision to forgo artificial food and water is a decision to commit active euthanasia." "Euthanasia Arguments," Christian Research Institute, http://www.equip.org/article/euthanasia-arguments/ (see the section entitled "Forgoing Artificial Air, Nutrition, and Hydration").

40. "Artificially-Administered Nutrition and Hydration," Christian Medical & Dental Associations, https://cmda.org/resources/publication/artificially-administered-nutrition-and-hydration-ethics-statement.

that nutrition and hydration should be continued unless it is harmful to the patient or clearly contrary to the patient's expressed wishes.

In addition, modern medicine should be used to alleviate the pain and suffering of a terminally-ill patient (see Matt. 7:12; 22:39). In the vast majority of cases today, medicines, especially morphine or drugs known as opioids, are available that will protect people from ongoing, extreme suffering as they near death.[41] A recent study found that those with advanced cancer who receive early palliative care to help with physical and emotional issues have a better quality of life and do not experience as much suffering as those who do not receive such care.[42]

C. ARGUMENTS AGAINST EUTHANASIA FROM REASON AND EVIDENCE APART FROM THE BIBLE

In addition to the arguments given above from Exodus 20:13 ("You shall not murder") and 2 Samuel 1:1–16 (the death of Saul), four additional arguments can be made against euthanasia:

1. The Human Moral Instinct That Murder Is Wrong.

Most people have a conviction that it is wrong to murder another human being. An argument can be made from

---

41. "Last Days of Life," National Institutes of Health, National Cancer Institute, www.cancer.gov/cancertopics/pdq/supportivecare/lasthours/Patient/page2#Keypoint7.

42. "Study Confirms Benefits of Early Palliative Care for Advanced Cancer," National Institutes of Health, National Cancer Institute, Oct. 5, 2016, https://www.cancer.gov/news-events/cancer-currents-blog/2016/palliative-care-quality.

this general conviction to the specific application that it is wrong to murder elderly or terminally-ill people. Is murder not murder whether the victim is young or old, strong or weak, or in good health or suffering? None of these considerations should affect the moral status of the person as a human being.

2. The Slippery Slope from Euthanasia to an "Obligation" to Die. Concerns about a "slippery slope" in public policy have some persuasive force. If euthanasia is allowed for *some* patients who are suffering, then how can we prevent it from being applied to *more and more* patients who are suffering? And with the increasing cost of health care for elderly and extremely ill patients, there is likely to be growing pressure on people to ask that their lives be taken. Moreover, "nations that have allowed for physician-assisted suicide find that a society can quickly move from merely *allowing* 'the right to die' to the belief that there is 'an *obligation* to die' on the part of the elderly and the very ill people who are 'draining resources' from the society. In such situations it becomes likely that a number of elderly people will be put to death against their will."[43]

3. The Horror of Involuntary Euthanasia. The situation in the Netherlands has become particularly notorious—a large number of elderly people have been put to death

---

43. "The End of Life," in *ESV Study Bible* (Wheaton, IL: Crossway, 2008), 2543. (I was the primary author of this article, which was also modified and approved by at least three other editors.)

against their will.[44] In 2012, 4,188 people were euthanized in the Netherlands through a mix of sedatives and a lethal dose of muscle relaxant.[45] Wesley Smith, an attorney for the International Anti-Euthanasia Task Force, has written that the number is actually much higher:

> The evidence of decades demonstrates that such involuntary euthanasia is rampant. Indeed, in its 1997 ruling refusing to create a constitutional right to assisted suicide (*Washington v. Glucksberg*) the United States Supreme Court quoted a 1991 Dutch government study finding that in 1990 doctors committed "more than 1000 cases of euthanasia without an explicit request" and "an additional 4,941 cases where physicians administered lethal morphine overdoses without the patients' explicit consent." That means in 1990, nearly 6,000 of approximately 130,000 people who died in the Netherlands that year were involuntarily euthanized—approximately 4 percent of all Dutch deaths. So much for "choice."[46]

Euthanasia advocate Philip Nitschke invented the so-called "peaceful pill" to induce suicide, and he also conducted "how to commit suicide" clinics. He said that his

---

44. A concise summary of the Netherlands' euthanasia law can be read at www .internationaltaskforce.org/hollaw.htm.

45. Bruno Waterfield, "Number of Dutch Killed by Euthanasia Rises by 13 Percent," *The Telegraph,* Sept. 24, 2013, http://www.telegraph.co.uk/news/world news/europe/netherlands/10330823/Number-of-Dutch-killed-by-euthanasia-rises -by-13-per-cent.html.

46. Wesley Smith, "We Ignore the Dutch Legalization of Euthanasia at Our Own Peril," Euthanasia.com, Dec. 17, 2000, http://www.euthanasia.com/nethcases.html.

personal position is that "if we believe that there is a right to life, then we must accept that people have a right to dispose of that life whenever they want."[47] He continued:

> Many people I meet and argue with believe that human life is sacred. I do not. . . . If you believe that your body belongs to God and that to cut short a life is a crime against God, then you will clearly not agree with my thoughts on this issue. I do not mind people holding these beliefs and suffering as much as they wish as they die. For them, redemptive suffering may well pry open heaven's door that little bit wider, and if that is their belief they are welcome to it, but I strongly object to having those views shoved down my neck. I want my belief—that human life is not sacred—accorded the same respect.[48]

The slippery slope has also extended into infant euthanasia. In September 2005 the Dutch government announced its intention to expand its euthanasia policy to allow doctors to end the lives of infants with the parents' consent. Under the "Gronican Protocol," euthanasia is allowed when it is decided that a child is terminally ill with no prospect of recovery and suffering great pain.[49]

Christine Rosen, author of *Preaching Eugenics*, says:

47. Quoted in Kathryn Jean Lopez, "Euthanasia Sets Sail: An interview with Philip Nitschke, the other 'Dr. Death,'" *National Review*, June 5, 2001, http://www.nationalreview.com/article/420133/euthanasia-sets-sail-kathryn-jean-lopez.

48. Quoted in Lopez, "Euthanasia Sets Sail."

49. Wesley J. Smith, "From Holland to New Jersey," *National Review*, March 22, 2005, http://www.nationalreview.com/article/213965/pushing-infanticide-wesley-j-smith.

The Netherlands' embrace of euthanasia has been a gradual process aided by the growing acceptance (in a much more secular Europe) that some life is "unworthy of life." Indeed, Europe is doing just that. According to the Associated Press, 73 percent of French doctors have admitted to using drugs to end an infant's life, with between 2 and 4 percent of doctors in the United Kingdom, Italy, Spain, Germany, and Sweden confessing the same.[50]

Belgium has also passed a law allowing the euthanasia of children, and the first child was killed in September 2016.[51] Under Belgium's law, children of any age can ask to be euthanized if they are deemed to have a terminal illness.[52] Former Alliance Defending Freedom (ADF) International attorney Roger Kiska, who led the legal fight against the law, said after its passage:

> No civilized society allows children to kill themselves. Far from a compassionate law, this law hands the equivalent of a loaded gun to a child with the astonishing belief that the child should be free to pull the trigger if he or she so chooses. Belgium's

---

50. Christine Rosen, *Preaching Eugenics: Religious Leaders and the American Eugenics Movement* (Oxford: Oxford University Press, 2004), cited in Kathryn Jean Lopez, "Mercy!" *National Review*, March 30, 2005, http://www.national review.com/article/214029/mercy-kathryn-jean-lopez

51. Yves Logghe, "First Child Dies by Legal Euthanasia in Belgium," CBS News, Sept. 19, 2016, http://www.cbsnews.com/news/child-dies-by-euthanasia-in -belgium-where-assistance-in-dying-is-legal/

52. Charlotte McDonald-Gibson, "Belgium Extends Euthanasia Law to Kids," *Time*, Feb. 13, 2014, http://time.com/7565/belgium-euthanasia-law-children -assisted-suicide/.

decision to allow this is grotesquely abhorrent and inhumane. As the legal analysis we provided to members of the Belgian Parliament explained, the law's underlying premise is that life is not worth living and that children are somehow mature enough to make such grave decisions about their own lives. On the contrary, this law exploits vulnerable children by handing to them a "freedom" that they are completely ill-equipped to bear.[53]

4. Examples of People Who Have Surprisingly Recovered. A final argument against euthanasia comes from personal narratives and testimonies from people who were apparently terminally ill or had life-threatening injuries but nevertheless recovered, as well as from elderly people who are still living happy, productive lives.

One example of this phenomenon is Jesse Ramirez of Mesa, Arizona. In May 2007, the 36-year-old Jesse was in a horrific automobile accident while he and his wife were engaged in an argument.[54] Ramirez suffered a broken neck and head trauma, and fell into a coma. Barely 10 days after the accident, Jesse's food, water, and antibiotics were withdrawn at the request of his wife, who received only minor injuries in the accident. He was then transferred to hospice care, where he would have died, but Alliance Defending Freedom attorneys, at the behest of Jesse's sister, were

---

53. "Belgium to Allow Children to Kill Themselves," Alliance Defending Freedom, Feb. 13, 2014, http://www.adfmedia.org/News/PRDetail/8847.

54. Dennis Wagner, "Injured Man's Awakening Called 'Miracle,'" *USA Today*, June 27, 2007, https://usatoday30.usatoday.com/news/nation/2007-06-26-comatose_n.htm.

successful in restoring food, water, and treatment. A few days later, Jesse came out of his coma. Although he went without food and water for six days, Jesse recovered and walked out of the hospital in October 2007, and continued his recovery at home.[55] In 2008 the state of Arizona passed "Jesse's Law," which closed a loophole in the decision-making process for patients who are physically unable to communicate their wishes regarding medical care.[56]

D. OBJECTIONS

There are three primary objections to the position opposing euthanasia that I have outlined above:

1. "We Must Uphold the Value of Human Freedom." Proponents of euthanasia often emphasize the importance of human freedom, even the freedom of an individual to choose to end his or her own life.

But if it is morally wrong to actively murder another person, then the fact that a person would *choose* to be murdered does not nullify this moral conclusion. There are many cases in which someone might so despair of life that he or she would say, "I want to die." But should we then say that it is right to murder such a person? If murder is morally wrong, even the desire of the person who wants to be murdered cannot make it morally right, for it is still

---

55. Rick Dubek, "Comatose Mesa Man Walks Out of Hospital," AZCentral, Oct. 19, 2007, http://archive.azcentral.com/12news/news/articles/jesseramirez walks10192007-CR.html.

56. "ADF Commends Signing of 'Jesse's Law,'" Alliance Defending Freedom, June 25, 2008, http://www.adfmedia.org/News/PRDetail/1907.

taking a human life. A person's right to life does not depend on the person himself wanting to live.

2. "Sometimes We Need to Alleviate Pain." Another objection is that some people are experiencing unbearable, unending pain, and they are often only a few months or years from death in any case.

However, pain and suffering are not sufficient reasons to overcome the moral prohibition against murder. A better solution is to alleviate the pain (which is almost always possible with modern medicine)[57] and do whatever else can be done to overcome the person's suffering.

3. "Medical Resources and Money Are Limited." A final argument is that money and medical resources are limited, and therefore we should put to death elderly or very ill people so that these resources are not wasted on them. This is not the question of allocating a scarce resource (say, a kidney transplant) to a younger or healthier person. Rather, it is the argument that older or very ill people *should not be using so much medical care at all.*

But this argument, phrased another way, essentially says that it is right to kill people whose care is costing us too much. This argument is simply a way of saying, "We don't have enough money to care for these elderly and terminally ill people." But is that a justification for taking another person's life? This would change the commandment "You

---

57. There are rare cases in which no significant relief from pain is possible with medication.

shall not murder" into a different commandment: "You shall not murder unless you do so to spend your money on something else." This objection is hardly acceptable on moral grounds.

I must emphasize that this is not the discussion about "letting die," which may be the right decision with terminally-ill patients who have no reasonable human hope of recovery. In such cases, the wishes of the patient and the financial resources available to care for the patient become genuine considerations. But here we are not talking about letting die. We are talking about whether it is right to *actively kill* another person because we think society should spend less on caring for old, sick people and direct more of its spending to other medical purposes. We are talking about whether it is right to murder.

It is important to realize that all three of these objections are based on a viewpoint that is contrary to a Christian worldview. These three objections do not value human life as something sacred, something that uniquely carries the image of God in this world. And they do not give full weight to the moral force of God's command "You shall not murder."

E. RECENT LEGAL TRENDS

Recent legal trends in at least some states in the United States seem to be moving in the direction of allowing more euthanasia. In most states, euthanasia is still prohibited and laws against murder apply to it. However, Oregon voters enacted the "Death with Dignity Act," what is called physician-assisted suicide, in 1994,[58] and this law was upheld by the U.S. Court of Appeals for the Ninth Circuit in 1997. The U.S. Supreme Court subsequently denied a request to hear an appeal of this decision. In a subsequent challenge contending that federal controlled-substances acts overrode the law, the U.S. Supreme Court ruled six to three in the law's favor in 2006.[59] In November 2008 the citizens of Washington state also legalized physician-assisted suicide.[60] In October 2015, Gov. Jerry Brown of California signed into law a bill that legalized assisted suicide in that state. The law went into effect on June 9, 2016.[61] Shortly thereafter, a health insurer refused to pay for chemotherapy for a woman suffering from terminal cancer, but agreed to pay for her less expensive suicide pills instead.[62] Assisted suicide is legal in Vermont and Montana as well.[63]

On the other hand, in 1999, Jack Kevorkian, a physician in Michigan, was convicted for assisting a patient to

---

58. See http://www.oregon.gov/oha/PH/PROVIDERPARTNERRESOURCES/EVALUATIONRESEARCH/DEATHWITHDIGNITYACT/pages/index.aspx.

59. Gonzales v. Oregon, 546 U.S. 243 (2006).

60. "Washington State to Allow Assisted Suicide," Associated Press, March 2, 2009, https://usatoday30.usatoday.com/news/nation/2009-03-01-washington-assisted_N.htm.

61. Lisa Aliferis, "California to Permit Medically Assisted Suicide as of June 9," National Public Radio, March 10, 2016, http://www.npr.org/sections/health-shots/2016/03/10/469970753/californias-law-on-medically-assisted-suicide-to-take-effect-june-9.

62. Bradford Richardson, "Assisted-suicide law prompts insurance company to deny coverage to terminally ill California woman," *Washington Times*, Oct. 20, 2016, http://www.washingtontimes.com/news/2016/oct/20/assisted-suicide-law-prompts-insurance-company-den/.

63. "'Death With Dignity' Laws By State," FindLaw, http://healthcare.findlaw.com/patient-rights/death-with-dignity-laws-by-state.html.

commit suicide in an act that was displayed on television and that violated current Michigan law.[64]

F. THE IMPORTANCE OF THIS ISSUE

The direction a society takes on the question of euthanasia is a reflection of how highly it values human life and how highly it values God's command not to murder. In societies where physician-assisted suicide becomes legal, it sets the stage for a further erosion of the protection of human life. Some people will be thought "too old" to deserve medical treatment. Compassion and care for the elderly will diminish, and they will be more and more thought of as burdens to be cared for rather than valuable members of the society.

And unless we experience premature death, all of us reading this chapter will ourselves one day be those "elderly" people who need care and support from others.

---

64. "Kevorkian Gets 10 to 25 Years in Prison," CNN, April 13, 1999, www.cnn .com/US/9904/13/kevorkian.03/.

G. APPENDIX: ARTIFICIALLY-ADMINISTERED NUTRITION AND HYDRATION

A statement of the Christian Medical & Dental Associations

A frequent ethical dilemma in contemporary medical practice is whether or not to employ artificial means to provide nutrition or hydration[65] in certain clinical situations. Legal precedents on this question do not always resolve the ethical dilemma or accord with Christian ethics. CMDA offers the following ethical guidelines to assist Christians in these difficult and often emotionally laden decisions. The following domains must be considered:

BIBLICAL

1. All human beings at every stage of life are made in God's image, and their inherent dignity must be treated with respect (Genesis 1:25–26). This applies in three ways:
   a. All persons or their surrogates should be given the opportunity to make their own medical decisions in as informed a manner as possible. Their unique values must be considered before the medical team gives their recommendations.
   b. The intentional taking of human life is wrong (Genesis 9:5–6; Exodus 20:13).

---

65. ANH may be given enterically through a nasogastric (NG) tube. Alternatively, a percutaneous gastrostomy tube (PEG) may be inserted endoscopically so that a feeding tube is passed through the abdominal wall. Total parenteral nutrition (TPN) is administered through a large bore catheter inserted into a central vein in the chest. Hydration (water plus electrolytes) may be given with nutrition in any of these ways or alone through a peripheral intravenous catheter or, less commonly, through a catheter inserted subcutaneously.

    c. Christians specifically (Matthew 25:35–40; James 2:15–17), and healthcare professionals in general, have a special obligation to protect the vulnerable.

2. Offering oral food and fluids for all people capable of being safely nourished or comforted by them, and assisting when necessary, is a moral requirement (Matthew 25:31–45).

3. All people are responsible to God for the care of their bodies, and healthcare professionals are responsible to God for the care of their patients. As Christians we understand that our bodies fundamentally belong to God; they are not our own (1 Corinthians 6:20).

4 We are to treat all people as we would want to be treated ourselves (Luke 6:31).

5. Technology should not be used only to prolong the dying process when death is imminent. There is "a time to die" (Ecclesiastes 3:2).

6. Death for a believer will lead to an eternal future in God's presence, where ultimate healing and fulfillment await (2 Corinthians 5:8; John 3:16, 6:40, 11:25–26, and 17:3).

7. Medical decisions must be made prayerfully and carefully. When faced with serious illness, patients may seek consultation with spiritual leaders, recognizing that God is the ultimate healer and source of wisdom (Exodus 15:26; James 1:5, 5:14).

8. Illness often provides a context in which the following biblical principles are in tension:

    a. God sovereignly uses the difficult experiences of life to accomplish his inscrutable purposes

(Job; 1 Peter 4:19; Romans 8:28; 2 Corinthians 12:9).

b. God desires his people to enjoy his gifts and to experience health and rest (Psalm 127:2; Matthew 11:28–29; Hebrews 4:11).

MEDICAL

1. Loving patient care should aim to minimize discomfort at the end of life. Dying without ANH need not be painful and in some situations can promote comfort.

    a. Nutrition: In the active stages of dying, as the body systems begin to shut down, the alimentary tract deteriorates to where it cannot process food, and forced feeding can cause discomfort and bloating. As a person can typically live for weeks without food, absence of nutrition in the short term does not equate with causing death.

    b. Hydration: In the otherwise healthy patient with reversible dehydration, deprivation of fluids causes symptoms of discomfort that may include thirst, fatigue, headache, rapid heart rate, agitation, and confusion. By contrast, most natural deaths occur with some degree of dehydration, which serves a purpose in preventing the discomfort of fluid overload. As the heart becomes weaker, if not for progressive dehydration, fluid would back up in the lungs, causing respiratory distress, or elsewhere in the body, causing excessive swelling of the tissues. In the dying patient, dehydration causes discomfort only if the lips and tongue are allowed to dry.

2. Complications of ANH.
   a. Tube feedings may increase the risk of pneumonia from aspiration of stomach contents.
   b. Tube feedings and medications administered through the tube may cause diarrhea, increasing the possibility of developing skin breakdown or bedsores, and infections, especially in an already debilitated patient.
   c. Patients with feeding tubes will, not infrequently, either willfully or in a state of confusion, pull at the feeding tube, causing damage to the skin at the insertion site or dislodging the tube. Prevention of harm may require otherwise unnecessary physical restraints or sedating medications.
   d. The surgical procedure of inserting a percutaneous gastrostomy (feeding) tube can occasionally lead to bowel perforation or other serious complications.
   e. Complications of TPN include those associated with the central venous catheter, such as blood vessel perforation or collapsed lung; local or blood stream infection; and complications associated with the feeding itself, such as fluid overload, electrolyte disturbances, labile blood glucose, liver dysfunction, or gall bladder disease.
3. Disease context.
   a. Cancer: End-stage cancer often increases the metabolic requirements of the body beyond the nutrition attainable by oral means. When the cancer has progressed to this stage, the patient may experience considerable pain, and ANH may only prolong dying.

    b. Severe neurologic impairment: This frequently has an indeterminate prognosis rendering decision making problematic. It requires a careful evaluation of the probability of improvement, the burdens and benefits of medical intervention, and a judgment of how much the patient can endure while awaiting the hoped-for improvement.

    c. Dementia: If a patient survives to the late stages of dementia, the ability to swallow food and fluids by mouth may be impaired or lost. ANH has been shown in rigorous scientific studies to improve neither comfort nor the length of life and may, in fact, shorten it.

ETHICAL

1. There is no ethical distinction between withdrawing and withholding ANH. However, the psychological impact may be different if withdrawal or withholding is perceived to have been the cause of death.

2. If there is uncertainty about the wisdom of employing ANH, a time-limited trial may be considered.

3. Any medical intervention should be undertaken only after a careful assessment of the expected benefit versus the potential burden.

4. The decision whether to implement or withdraw ANH is based on a consideration of medical circumstances, values, and expertise, and involves the patient or designated surrogate in partnership with the healthcare team.

5. It is best that all stakeholders strive for consensus.

SOCIAL

1. Eating is a social function. Even for compromised patients unable to feed themselves, being fed by others provides some of the best opportunities they have for meaningful human contact and pleasure.
2. People suffering from advanced dementia frequently remain sentient and social.

CMDA endorses ethical guidelines in four categories:

1. **Strong indications:** Situations where the use of ANH is strongly indicated and it would be unethical for a medical team to decline to recommend it or deny its implementation. Examples of these situations would be:
   a. A patient with inability to take oral fluids and nutrition for anatomic or functional reasons with a high probability of reversing in a timely manner.
   b. A patient who is in a stable condition with a disease that is not deemed to be progressive or terminal and the patient or surrogate desires life prolongation (e.g., an individual born unable to swallow but who is otherwise viable, or the victim of trauma or cancer who has had curative surgery but cannot take oral feedings).
   c. A patient with a newly-diagnosed but not imminently fatal severe brain impairment in the absence of other life-threatening comorbidities.
   d. Gastrointestinal tract failure or the medical need for total bowel rest may justify the use of TPN in some contexts not otherwise terminal.

e. An otherwise terminal patient who requests short-term ANH, fully informed of the risk being taken, to allow him or her to experience an important life event.

2. **Allowable indications:** Situations where the use of ANH is morally neutral and the patient or surrogate should be encouraged to make the best decision possible after the medical team has provided as much education as necessary. Examples of these situations would be:

a. A patient with severe, progressive neurologic impairment who otherwise desires that life be prolonged (e.g., end-stage amyotrophic lateral sclerosis).

b. Conditions that would not be terminal if ANH were provided but, in the opinion of either the patient or surrogate, there is uncertainty whether the anticipated benefits versus burdens justify the intervention.

3. **Not recommended but allowable:** Situations where the use of ANH may not be recommended in all instances but, depending on the clinical context, would be morally licit, assuming the patient or surrogate has been informed of the benefits and potential complications and requests that it be initiated or continued. Examples of these situations would be:

a. A patient who has a disease state, such as a major neurologic disability, where, after several months of support and observation, the prognosis for recovery of consciousness or communication remains poor or indeterminate. In cases where ANH is withdrawn or withheld, oral fluids should still be offered to the patient who expresses thirst.

b. A patient whose surrogate requests overruling the patient's advance directive and medical team's recommendation against ANH because of the particular or changing clinical context.

c. Placement of a PEG in a patient who is able but compromised in the ability to take oral feeding as a convenient substitute for the sometimes time-consuming process of oral feeding, for ease of medication administration, or to satisfy eligibility criteria for transfer from an acute-care setting to an appropriate level of short-term nursing care, long-term care, or a rehabilitation facility. ANH decisions in such cases should consider the potential benefits versus risks and burdens of available feeding options, the capacity of caregivers to administer feedings, and prudent stewardship of medical and financial resources, always in regard to the best interest of the patient.

4. **Unallowable indications:** Situations where it is unethical to employ ANH. Examples of these situations would include:

a. Using ANH in a patient against the patient's or surrogate's expressed wishes, either extemporaneously or as indicated in an advance directive and agreed to by the surrogate. There may be particular medical contexts in which a surrogate may overrule an advance directive that requests ANH on the basis of substituted judgment if the surrogate knows the patient would not want it in the present context.

b. Compelling a medical professional to be involved in the insertion of a feeding tube or access for TPN in violation of his or her conscience. In this situation the requesting medical professional must be willing to transfer the care of the patient to another who will provide the service. (See CMDA statement on Healthcare Right of Conscience.)

c. Using ANH in a situation where it is biologically futile, as in a patient declared to be brain dead. An exception would be the brain dead pregnant patient in which the purpose of ANH is to preserve viable fetal life; ANH in this circumstance is not futile for the life in the womb.

d. Using ANH in an attempt to delay the death of an imminently dying patient (except in the context in 1.e. above).

CMDA recognizes that ANH is a controversial issue with indistinct moral boundaries. Disagreements should be handled in the spirit of Christian love, showing respect to all.

Unanimously approved by the House of Representatives
April 21, 2016
Ridgecrest, North Carolina[66]

---

66. Reproduced with permission from the website of the Christian Medical & Dental Associations, https://www.cmda.org/resources/publication/artificially-administered-nutrition-and-hydration-ethics-statement.

QUESTIONS FOR PERSONAL APPLICATION

Abortion:

1. How did this book affect your thinking about abortion?

2. If you have ever had an abortion or have encouraged someone else to have an abortion, have you asked God's forgiveness? Do you feel forgiven by him?

3. Is there anything that friends can do to help comfort someone who has had an abortion?

4. What are some practical ways in which Christians can help women who are dealing with an unwanted pregnancy?

5. Under what circumstances (if any) do you think abortion would be morally permissible?

6. Do you think that your government should have any laws prohibiting abortion? What do you think those laws should prohibit? What should they allow?

7. What character traits would be helpful for women who are experiencing an unexpected or unwanted pregnancy? For their friends and loved ones who want to encourage them?

Euthanasia:

1. How has this book affected the way you think about euthanasia?

2. If the time should come when you are experiencing a terminal illness and you have no reasonable

human hope of recovery, what kinds of medical treatments would you want done for you for the purpose of prolonging your life? For the purpose of alleviating your pain?

3. Have you talked with members of your immediate family about your wishes regarding end-of-life care? Have you put these wishes in a written document that will be legally recognized, such as (in the United States) a "medical power of attorney" document? (See further discussion in Grudem, *Christian Ethics*, 641–42.)

4. What character traits would be especially helpful for people going through a terminal illness? For the members of their families who are close to them?

SPECIAL TERMS

abortion
assisted suicide
euthanasia
killing
letting die
nutrition and hydration
slippery slope

BIBLIOGRAPHY

Sections in Christian Ethics Texts

Clark, David K., and Robert V. Rakestraw, eds. *Readings in Christian Ethics*. 2 vols. Grand Rapids, MI: Baker, 1994, 2:21–56; 2:95–138.

Davis, John Jefferson. *Evangelical Ethics: Issues Facing the Church Today*. 4th ed. Phillipsburg, NJ: P&R, 2015, 131–60; 161–97.

Feinberg, John S., and Paul D. Feinberg. *Ethics for a Brave New World*. 2nd ed. Wheaton, IL: Crossway, 2010, 63–155; 157–226.

Frame, John M. *The Doctrine of the Christian Life: A Theology of Lordship*. Phillipsburg, NJ: P&R, 2008, 717–32; 734–38.

Geisler, Norman L. *Christian Ethics: Contemporary Issues and Options*. 2nd ed. Grand Rapids, MI: Baker, 2010, 131–59; 160–79.

Grudem, Wayne. *Christian Ethics: An Introduction to Biblical Moral Reasoning*. Wheaton, IL: Crossway, 2018, 566–86; 587–605.

Gushee, David P., and Glen H. Stassen. *Kingdom Ethics: Following Jesus in Contemporary Context*. 2nd ed. Grand Rapids, MI: Eerdmans, 2016, 418–28; 434–41.

Hays, Richard B. *The Moral Vision of the New Testament: Community, Cross, New Creation: A Contemporary Introduction to New Testament Ethics*. San Francisco: HarperSanFrancisco, 1996, 444–61.

Jones, David Clyde. *Biblical Christian Ethics*. Grand Rapids, MI: Baker, 1994, 11–16.

Kaiser, Walter C., Jr. *What Does the Lord Require? A Guide for Preaching and Teaching Biblical Ethics*. Grand Rapids, MI: Baker, 2009, 105–16; 139–50.

McQuilkin, Robertson, and Paul Copan. *An Introduction to Biblical Ethics: Walking in the Way of Wisdom*. 3rd ed. Downers Grove, IL: InterVarsity Press, 2014, 363–82; 387–93.

Rae, Scott B. *Moral Choices: An Introduction to Ethics*. 3rd ed. Grand Rapids, MI: Zondervan, 2009, 121–43; 212–46.

Other Works

Alcorn, Randy. *Does the Birth Control Pill Cause Abortion?* 7th ed. Gresham, OR: Eternal Perspective Ministries, 2004.

Alcorn, Randy. *ProLife Answers to ProChoice Arguments*. 2nd ed. Sisters, OR: Multnomah, 2000.

Alcorn, Randy. *Why Pro-Life? Caring for the Unborn and Their Mothers*. Revised and updated ed. Peabody, MA: Hendrickson, 2012.

Beckwith, Francis J. *Politically Correct Death: Answering the Arguments for Abortion Rights*. Grand Rapids, MI: Baker, 1993.

Best, Megan. *Fearfully and Wonderfully Made: Ethics and the Beginning of Human Life*. Kingsford, NSW, Australia: Matthias Media, 2012.

Cameron, N. M. de S. "Euthanasia." In *New Dictionary of Christian Ethics and Pastoral Theology*, edited by David J. Atkinson and David H. Field, 357–59. Leicester, UK: InterVarsity, and Downers Grove, IL: InterVarsity Press, 1995.

Cook, E. D. "Abortion." In *New Dictionary of Christian Ethics and Pastoral Theology*, 131–34.

Frame, John M. *Medical Ethics: Principles, Persons, and Problems*. Christian Perspectives. Phillipsburg, NJ: Presbyterian and Reformed, 1988.

Ganz, Richard L., and C. Everett Koop, eds. *Thou Shalt Not Kill: The Christian Case against Abortion.* New Rochelle, NY: Arlington House, 1978.

George, Robert P., and Christopher Tollefsen. *Embryo: A Defense of Human Life.* New York: Doubleday, 2008.

Gorman, Michael J. *Abortion and the Early Church: Christian, Jewish and Pagan Attitudes in the Greco-Roman World.* Eugene, OR: Wipf & Stock, 1998.

Hekman, Randall J. *Justice for the Unborn: Why We Have "Legal" Abortion and How We Can Stop It.* Ann Arbor, MI: Servant, 1984.

Hensley, Jeff Lane, ed. *The Zero People: Essays on Life.* Ann Arbor, MI: Servant, 1983.

Kilner, John Frederic. *Life on the Line: Ethics, Aging, Ending Patients' Lives, and Allocating Vital Resources.* Grand Rapids, MI: Eerdmans, 1992.

Kilner, John Frederic, ed. *Why the Church Needs Bioethics: A Guide to Wise Engagement with Life's Challenges.* Grand Rapids, MI: Zondervan, 2011.

Kilner, John Frederic, Arlene B. Miller, and Edmund D. Pellegrino, eds. *Dignity and Dying: A Christian Appraisal.* Horizons in Bioethics Series. Carlisle, UK: Paternoster, 1996.

Kilner, John Frederic, and C. Ben Mitchell. *Does God Need Our Help? Cloning, Assisted Suicide, and Other Challenges in Bioethics.* Vital Questions. Wheaton, IL: Tyndale, 2003.

Klusendorf, Scott. *The Case for Life: Equipping Christians to Engage the Culture.* Wheaton, IL: Crossway, 2009.

Kreeft, Peter. *The Unaborted Socrates: A Dramatic Debate on the Issues Surrounding Abortion*. Downers Grove, IL: InterVarsity Press, 1983.

Mitchell, C. Ben. *Biotechnology and the Human Good*. Washington, DC: Georgetown University Press, 2007.

Mitchell, C. Ben, and D. Joy Riley. *Christian Bioethics: A Guide for Pastors, Health Care Professionals, and Families*. B&H Studies in Christian Ethics. Nashville: B&H Academic, 2014.

Olasky, Marvin N. *Abortion Rites: A Social History of Abortion in America*. Wheaton, IL: Crossway, 1992.

Piper, John. *Brothers, We Are Not Professionals: A Plea to Pastors for Radical Ministry*. In The Collected Works of John Piper, edited by David Mathis and Justin Taylor, vol. 3, 137–432. Wheaton, IL: Crossway, 2017. See "Brothers, Blow the Trumpet for the Unborn," 390–403.

Piper, John. "'Rescue Those Being Led Away to Death': A Defense of Trespassing Abortion Clinics When Life Is at Stake [1989]." In The Collected Works of John Piper, vol. 12, 339–45.

Platt, David. "Modern Holocaust: The Gospel and Abortion." In *Counter Culture: Following Christ in an Anti-Christian Age*, revised and updated ed., 59–80. Carol Stream, IL: Tyndale Momentum, 2017.

Tada, Joni Eareckson. *When Is It Right to Die? Suicide, Euthanasia, Suffering, Mercy*. Grand Rapids, MI: Zondervan, 1992.

Taylor, Justin. "'Abortion Is about God': Piper's Passionate, Prophetic Pro-Life Preaching." In *For the Fame of God's*

Name: Essays in Honor of John Piper, edited by Sam Storms and Justin Taylor, 328–50. Wheaton, IL: Crossway, 2010.

Taylor, Justin. "Abortion: Why Silence and Inaction Are Not Options for Evangelicals." In *Don't Call It a Comeback: The Same Faith for a New Day*, edited by Kevin DeYoung, 179–90. Wheaton, IL: Crossway, 2011.

Tollefsen, Christopher O., Patrick Lee, and Robert P. George. "Marco Rubio Is Right: The Life of a New Human Being Begins at Conception." *Public Discourse*, Aug. 5, 2015, http://www.thepublicdiscourse.com/2015/08/15520/.

VanDrunen, David. *Bioethics and the Christian Life: A Guide to Making Difficult Decisions*. Wheaton, IL: Crossway, 2009.

SCRIPTURE MEMORY PASSAGES

Luke 1:44: For behold, when the sound of your greeting came to my ears, the baby in my womb leaped for joy.

Exodus 20:13: You shall not murder.

HYMNS

"Does Jesus Care?"

Does Jesus care when my heart is pained
Too deeply for mirth and song;
As the burdens press, and the cares distress,
And the way grows weary and long?

Refrain:
O yes, He cares, I know He cares!
His heart is touched with my grief;

When the days are weary, the long nights dreary,
I know my Savior cares.

Does Jesus care when my way is dark
With a nameless dread and fear?
As the daylight fades into deep night shades,
Does He care enough to be near?

Does Jesus care when I've tried and failed
To resist some temptation strong;
When for my deep grief I find no relief,
Tho my tears flow all night long?

Does Jesus care when I've said goodbye
To the dearest on earth to me,
And my sad heart aches til it nearly breaks—
Is it aught to Him? Does He see?

Author: Frank E. Graeff, 1860–1919

"Great Is Thy Faithfulness"

Great is Thy faithfulness, O God my Father!
There is no shadow of turning with Thee;
Thou changest not, Thy compassions, they fail not:
As Thou hast been Thou forever wilt be.

Refrain:
Great is Thy faithfulness! Great is Thy faithfulness!
Morning by morning new mercies I see;
All I have needed Thy hand hath provided
Great is Thy faithfulness, Lord unto me!

Summer and winter, and springtime and harvest,
Sun, moon and stars in their courses above,
Join with all nature in manifold witness
To Thy great faithfulness, mercy and love.

Pardon for sin and a peace that endureth,
Thine own dear presence to cheer and to guide,
Strength for today and bright hope for tomorrow
Blessings all mine, with ten thousand beside![67]

Author: Thomas O. Chisholm, 1866–1960

General Index

Scripture Index